What a Touchy Subject!

Religious Liberty and Church-State Separation

J. BRENT WALKER

Walter B. and Kay W. Shurden Lectures
on Religious Liberty and Separation of Church and State
April 9-10, 2013

© 2014

Published in the United States by Nurturing Faith Inc., Macon GA,
www.nurturingfaith.net.

Library of Congress Cataloging-in-Publication Data is available.

ISBN 978-1-938514-54-8

Contents

Appendix

Foreword

By Walter B. Shurden

No Baptist leader in this country is more important to more people in this country than J. Brent Walker. Educated in both law and theology, Brent Walker is one of the most trusted voices in America on issues of religious freedom. No church-state issue in this republic evades his fair, even-handed, but scrutinizing mind. He is passionate about applying the United States Constitution and the Golden Rule to the knotty issues of the relationship of religion to government. He is my default setting for understanding how to untie these knots.

Brent is the executive director of the Baptist Joint Committee for Religious Liberty (BJC) in Washington, D.C. And the BJC is, in my opinion, one of the most important religious organizations in this country.

The "Joint" part of the name of the BJC reflects the fact that some fifteen different Baptist denominational organizations work together to support the work of the BJC.

The "Baptist" part of the name of the BJC can be terribly misleading. The BJC is no narrow sectarian denominational bureaucracy, selfishly protecting a single denomination's interests. The BJC is enormously significant for every citizen of the United States, whether Baptist or Buddhist, Methodist or Muslim, Assembly of God or atheist, Catholic or Congregationalist, liberal or fundamentalist, Republican or Democrat.

Why is the BJC so important? Because its passionate mission "is to defend and extend God-given religious liberty for all." ALL! 100%! EVERYONE! The BJC works long and hard and tirelessly for your freedom and the freedom of your children and grandchildren, whoever you are. And the BJC operates from the Baptist conviction that "religion must be freely exercised, neither advanced nor inhibited by government."

The First Amendment to the Constitution of the United States asserts that "Congress shall make no law respecting an establishment of religion, or prohibiting the free exercise thereof; or abridging the freedom of speech, or of the press; or the right of the people peaceably to assemble, and to petition the Government for a redress of grievances." The initial statement of this amendment boldly asserts that religious freedom is the "first freedom" of the American people. The BJC stands guard, defending the first freedom of the First Amendment.

In the following chapters, Brent Walker identifies the historical and theological principles that undergird freedom of religion. In doing so, he challenges the myth that religious freedom and church-state separation are rooted *only* in the ideas of the Enlightenment. Religious persons with spiritual convictions preceded the Enlightenment years, though most Enlightenment leaders certainly embraced and advocated religious freedom.

While some persons in the contemporary debate argue that the Establishment Clause ("Congress shall make no law respecting an establishment of religion") of the First Amendment intended only to prevent a single national church or showing preferences among faith groups, Walker passionately disagrees. The founders, he argues, utilized specific and expansive language to keep the new federal government from making laws regarding an establishment of religion generally.

Here are other significant points that Brent Walker makes in these chapters:

- The First Amendment and the entire Bill of Rights are "counter-majoritarian." They protect minorities from majority vote.
- A proper understanding of religious freedom requires government to facilitate religion without advancing it.
- The Free Exercise Clause of the First Amendment keeps government from hurting religion, while the Establishment Clause keeps government from trying to help religion.
- Brent's golden rule of church-state relations says, "I cannot ask government to promote my religion if I don't want government

to promote somebody else's religion; and I cannot permit government to hinder somebody else's religion if I don't want government to hinder my religion."

- The separation of church and state does not mandate a complete segregation of religion from public life, but danger always lurks when we try to combine religion and politics.
- When religion engages political issues, it should advance the common good, not a narrow sectarian agenda.

You hold in your hand one of the best primers to church-state issues that you will ever read. And Walker's words are readable, not obscured by arcane legal or theological language.

I am delighted that these chapters were first delivered as the Walter B. and Kay W. Shurden Lectures on Religious Liberty and Separation of Church and State.

—*Walter B. Shurden*
Minister at Large
Mercer University

Preface

The following presentations comprised the 2013 Walter B. and Kay W. Shurden Lectures on Religious Liberty and Separation of Church and State, delivered on the campus of Stetson University in DeLand, Florida, April 9-10. The introduction and first lecture were delivered during the same presentation, and the other two lectures were separate addresses.

The Shurdens endowed the annual event in 2004, making a $100,000 gift to the Baptist Joint Committee for Religious Liberty. Each year, a speaker delivers the lectures at a college campus to educate, inspire, and call others to an ardent commitment to religious freedom. The previous lecturers and locations are listed in the appendix.

These annual lectures are the product of Buddy and Kay Shurden's astonishing generosity and infectious passion for preserving religious liberty. As former professors, the Shurdens know firsthand the critical importance of connecting with students and other young people in particular to make sure tomorrow's leaders appreciate the vital importance of protecting this freedom today and into the future.

I was honored to be the eighth lecturer in this series. My presentations seek to clear up common, and often controversial, misconceptions regarding church-state issues. Some citations have been added to the lectures printed in this volume, but the text remains substantially as prepared and spoken on the Stetson University campus.

—*J. Brent Walker*
January 2014

Lectures

Introduction

Religious Liberty and Church-State Separation:
What a Touchy Subject!

I am reminded of a *Calvin and Hobbes* cartoon in which the first frame shows Calvin at his desk in class raising his hand frantically. After he is called on by the teacher, he says: "Miss Wormwood, I'm a fierce advocate of the separation of church and state. Nevertheless, I feel the need for spiritual guidance and comfort as I face the day's struggles. So, I was wondering if I could strip down, smear myself with paste, and set fire to this little effigy of you in a non-denominational sort of way." Then in the next frame you see Calvin marching off to the principal's office saying, "Boy, what a touchy subject!"

Yes, both religious liberty and separation of church and state *are* touchy subjects. That's because they go to matters of the heart, to our faith in God or not, and the dizzying diversity of religious expression we find in this country. They go also to what it means to be an American citizen and how we negotiate our political differences in a country nowadays that is all too either red or blue, and not sufficiently purple—not only states, but also neighborhoods, clubs, churches, and even TV shows!

Religious liberty and separation of church and state are also touchy because they are so commonly misunderstood.

I hope in these lectures to shed some light on this touchy subject and to clear up some misconceptions that exacerbate what are perceived to be great differences in our understanding and appreciation of this very important topic.

In the first lecture, titled "First Principles: God-Given, But Government Protected," I want to explore theological and historical underpinnings to the topic. I shall talk about some generative ideas in our Baptist heritage and in American history that serve to inform our understanding of religious liberty, and the critical importance of an institutional and functional separation between church and state to ensure that freedom's viability.

In the second lecture, titled "First Freedom: Accommodate Religion, But Don't Advance It," I shall move beyond the theological and historical realms to talk about constitutional aspects. Having discussed first *principles*, I want to talk about the first *freedom*—that is, the two religion clauses in the First Amendment that protect religious liberty are also "first" because they are listed in the first sixteen words—ahead of the all-important protections for freedom of speech, press, petition, and assembly. I plan to emphasize the importance of having a strong Free Exercise Clause and a strong Establishment Clause, the limits to the accommodation of religion by government, and then some current issues we face at the Baptist Joint Committee—both in Washington, D.C., and around our nation.

Lecture three is titled "Religion and Politics: How Did We Do in 2012?" I shall shift our focus from the First Amendment to Article VI of the Constitution and its prohibition on religious tests for public office. I plan to unpack how we go about upholding the separation of church and state and affirming the absolute relevance of religion to public life, while seeking to honor the letter and spirit of the ban on religious tests. Then, I want to see how we did in this regard in the 2012 election cycle.

Lecture 1

First Principles:
God-Given, But Government Protected

L et us look initially to first principles or that which lay in the backdrop of our understanding of religious liberty and church-state separation in contemporary American life. To my way of thinking, this needs to be examined theologically and historically both in Baptist life and in other venues, including late eighteenth-century American history.

I should say, especially with respect to this lecture, much of what I know and most of what I say will sound familiar to Buddy Shurden, because I have sat at his feet and imbibed his wisdom for years. I may not cite chapter and verse in great detail, but just know that Buddy could give this lecture today as well as I.

What informs my understanding of the proper relationship between church and state is a conviction that religious liberty is nothing less than a gift from God, not the result of any act of toleration or concession on the part of government. One of the reasons Baptists have always championed religious freedom—for others as much as for themselves—flows from their understanding of Scripture. Although we do not find many specific proof texts, there are pervasive principles and suggestive inferences throughout the Bible.[1]

Our conception of religious liberty flows naturally, first, from the nature of God. God is sovereign. As such, God ordained government but did not delegate plenary authority to human institutions. God is seen throughout the Scriptures as a liberating deity who loves his children and cares about that relationship enough to create us free to say "no." God wants a personal relationship with us; God does not want to control us like puppets. Hence, God is sovereign, free, personal, and loving.

It also inheres in the condition of humanity. God created humans in God's image (Gen. 1:26-27). Whatever else the doctrine of the *Imago Dei* means, it suggests at least that we have been created by God free to respond or not (response-able). This is what we Baptists have for more than 400 years called "soul freedom"—that God-infused liberty of conscience we all enjoy, simply because of who God is and who we are and how God has chosen to create and relate to us. Even though made in God's image, humans are still sinful and cannot be trusted completely to exercise absolute authority—particularly in government and other coercive institutions. One does not have to be a thorough-going Calvinist, as I surely am not, to understand the fallen nature of human institutions. One only needs to read the newspaper.

The nature of God and condition of humanity, and finally, the imperative of faith support religious liberty. For faith to be authentic, it must be free. Faith cannot be forced and be genuine at the same time. Coerced faith is an oxymoron. Jesus, for example, did not chase after the rich young man in Mark 10:17-22 when he declined to sell all that he had and give it to the poor, but instead Jesus let him go away "sorrowful." Yes, Jesus knocks, but he will never ever kick down the door (Rev. 3:20).

And, the teachings of Jesus as much as his actions inform our understanding. One of the best-known stories is the encounter between Jesus and those two most unlikely of allies: the Herodians and the Pharisees (Matt. 22:15-22). Their mutual disdain for Jesus bridged their divisions and caused them to ask him a question that was bound to get him into hot water: "Is it lawful to pay taxes to Caesar?"

If Jesus said yes, his credibility with the Jews would be shot; if he said no, the Romans would charge him with sedition. Either way, Jesus would lose. But, of course, Jesus avoided their snare; he would not be trapped. He said, "[R]ender to Caesar the things that are Caesar's and to God the things that are God's."

Now, Jesus was not articulating a constitutional doctrine here, nor was he referring to a wall of separation between church and state 1,600 years before Roger Williams talked about it. Rather, he was noting the existence of these two kingdoms to which we owe different duties and responsibilities. But his lesson does lay the theological foundation for a constitutional doctrine two millennia hence.

The apostle Paul announced the centrality of freedom time after time. Yes, he was often talking about freedom from sin or freedom from legalism, but his ringing words in Galatians—that for responsible freedom Christ has set us free—are at least congenial with the more modern notion of freedom from governmental interference (Gal. 5:1, 13-14). And, at least for Trinitarian believers, Paul's announcement that "Where the spirit of the Lord is, there is freedom" clearly makes God present in freedom (2 Cor. 3:17). A very liberating thought!

Finally, the language "whosoever will ..." that we find in many places in the Scriptures is a pervasive theme throughout the Bible, particularly in the New Testament (Matt. 16:25, Mark 8:34, Luke 9:24, Rev. 22:17). "Whosoever will ..." implies voluntary religion, through and through, and free will.

Yes, Baptists became champions of religious liberty and church-state separation in large measure because we are people of the Book. Early Baptists did not set out to discover "Baptist distinctives"; rather they happened upon them, first, by studying the Bible. Baptists also valued religious freedom and church-state separation because they suffered hard lessons of history. Their understanding was not academic; it was existential.

Early Baptists experienced firsthand the pain of persecution—the heartache and bloodshed occasioned by religious zealots armed with the coercive power of government. From jail cells in England to stockades in Massachusetts Bay to whipping posts in Virginia, the historical litany is familiar to many of our ears.

After establishing the first Baptist church on English soil, Thomas Helwys (c. 1575-1616) wrote a seminal treatise on religious liberty, *A Short Declaration of the Mystery of Iniquity* (1612), and sent a copy to King James I. In his inscription, Helwys wrote: "The king is a mortal man and not God, and therefore hath no power over the immortal souls of his subjects to make laws and ordinances for them and to set spiritual Lords over them."[2] For his trouble, Helwys, along with his wife, Joan, was severely persecuted. They later died in London's Newgate Prison.

Often called the apostle of religious liberty, Roger Williams (c. 1603-1683) came from England to Massachusetts Bay in 1631 preaching and teaching "soul freedom"—the notion that faith could not be dictated by any government authority, but must be nurtured freely and expressed directly to God. He advocated a "hedge or wall of separation between the garden of the church and the wilderness of the world."[3] We often give that line to Thomas Jefferson, but really it came from Williams a century and a half before. The theocrats in Massachusetts were so offended that they kicked Williams out of the colony. He trekked to what would become Rhode Island and founded a city he called "Providence" because he judged that God's providence had directed him there. Williams began that "livlie experiment" in religious liberty and founded the first Baptist church in North America.

Obadiah Holmes (1610-1682), also banished from Massachusetts because of his Baptist beliefs, settled in Newport, Rhode Island, seeking religious freedom. In 1651, Holmes, along with John Clarke and John Crandall, traveled back to Massachusetts to visit an aged and blind friend. After taking Communion in the friend's home, they were arrested for engaging in unlawful worship. Holmes was convicted and sentenced to a fine or whipping. When he refused to pay the fine because of conscience, he was "well whipped" with thirty lashes. As his punishment was being administered, Holmes was reported to have told his tormentors, "It is as if you have struck me with roses."[4] After his release, Holmes returned to Newport and served as a pastor for thirty years.

An evangelist preaching in Virginia during the heady decade of the 1780s, John Leland (1754-1841) boldly advocated religious liberty and the separation of church and state. He played a pivotal role in convincing our nation's founders of the need for specific guarantees protecting religious freedom in the Bill of Rights. He stood toe-to-toe with the likes of James Madison, Thomas Jefferson, and George Mason and never backed down on the way to the Bill of Rights. He later returned to his native Massachusetts where he continued to speak out in favor of religious liberty and against state-established religion.

Isaac Backus (1724-1806) was a Baptist freedom fighter, preacher, social activist, and a popular pamphleteer. A contemporary of (but thirty years older than) John Leland, Backus has been called "the most forceful and effective writer America produced on behalf of the pietistic or evangelical theory of the separation of church and state."[5] Backus agreed with Leland that government should not tax its citizens to support the teaching of religion and that the government had no power or authority over the church.

This pantheon of early Baptist freedom fighters—I could name a dozen more—testifies to the Baptist heritage of blazing trails for religious liberty. Such a cloud of witnesses inspires modern-day advocates in general and Baptists in particular for truth-telling to the powers that be in defending religious liberty and the separation of church and state. Hundreds of years separate these witnesses, but time has not silenced their voices.

Against this backdrop of centuries of religious persecution and intolerance in England and in most of the colonies, our nation's founders assembled in New York in 1789 to adopt a Bill of Rights to the new Constitution. Our forebears understood that when religious zeal is combined with a coercive power of the state, consciences are violated and persecution often results.

Old practices die hard. Yes, Puritans came to New England in search of religious freedom. But what they gained for themselves, they denied to others, such as Roger Williams and Quaker Mary Dyer. Moreover, all but four colonies—Rhode Island, Pennsylvania, New Jersey, and Delaware—had officially established churches and engaged in varying degrees of persecution and intolerance. All but two had religious qualifications for office, five denied basic civil rights to Catholics, and several made blasphemy a capital offense.

But the wise architects of our republic had a different vision for the new national government. The Constitution, adopted in 1787 in Philadelphia, never mentioned Christianity and spoke of religion only once when in Article VI it banned any "religious test" as a qualification for public office. With the adoption of the First

Amendment's religion clauses in the Bill of Rights ("Congress shall make no law respecting an establishment of religion, or prohibiting the free exercise thereof"), our founders made clear that one's status in the civil community would not depend on a willingness to sign on the dotted line of any religious confession.

Religious liberty is often called our "first freedom," both because of a widespread conviction that religious liberty was nothing less than a gift from God and because it was the first right ensured in the First Amendment. Both religion clauses were inserted to protect that religious liberty, but in different ways. The Establishment Clause keeps government from advancing or privileging religion and from violating the consciences of those who have no religious belief. The Free Exercise Clause keeps government from burdening or interfering with religious practice unless government can assert some paramount interest such as peace, safety, or public health and welfare. Both clauses were intended to keep government neutral, disengaging from religion to allow people of faith to practice their religion as they see fit.

It is important to recognize that the children of God and sons of the Enlightenment worked together in the late eighteenth century to develop governmental institutions that would protect what the former believed to be a gift from God and the latter a natural right of conscience. And, I do not think either could have done it without the help of the other. William R. Estep, a Baptist historian from a generation ago, so ably told us that the First Amendment's protection for religious liberty was adopted because of the support of the so-called "twice born" evangelical dissenters of the late eighteenth century—Baptists, Presbyterians, and Quakers.[6]

No less a scholar than conservative jurist and professor Michael W. McConnell understands the importance of this partnership. Seeing it fueled by the First Great Awakening (1720-1740), the drive for religious freedom and church-state separation was integral to the evangelical movement. McConnell notes:

> [T]he evangelical position ultimately coalesced with the secular liberal position, as against the dying tradition of civic republicanism. This explains why more

fervent evangelicals, including Baptists, tended to become Jeffersonians, notwithstanding the deism of Jefferson and the piety of his opponents. Religion, the evangelicals believed, is vital to civic harmony. But voluntary religious societies—not the state—are the best and only legitimate institutions for the transmission of religious faith and, with it, virtue.[7]

Permit me a brief sidebar here. Some today in the religious community, even the progressive Baptist community, see our current drive to perpetuate religious freedom and church-state separation to be rooted *only* in the Enlightenment, not theology or biblical principles. I hope that my remarks here dispel that canard. Baptists "got it" long before the Enlightenment thinkers came upon it. Thomas Helwys predated John Locke by nearly a century. Roger Williams preceded the Enlightenment thinkers of the late eighteenth century by at least 150 years. Even in modern times and post-modern days, Baptists and other people of faith who advocate for religious freedom and the separation of church and state continue to find their moorings in the Bible as much as, if not more than, in secular notions of the contours of freedom, however important they are.

Our nation's founders, supported by our Baptist forebears and, yes, armed with Enlightenment values, in my view, wanted to ensconce robust protection for religious liberty. That is to say, they intended to write a strong establishment clause and a strong free exercise clause.

It is a dicey enterprise to try to judge the "original intent" of our founders. First of all, there is no monolithic "intent." There were many "intents." And even conceding that point, intents are hard to pin down and translate into common practice. Our founders were politicians—smart, well-educated, well-intentioned to be sure—but still politicians. Whatever their intentions, the words in the First Amendment and the surrounding history that we can evaluate lead me to conclude that they intended a strong protection for religious freedom.

Some say that the Establishment Clause was intended only to keep the federal government from setting up a single national church or showing preference among faith groups, but not from aiding all religions generally. I think they are wrong. If all the founders wanted to do was simply to ban a single, official national church, they did not do a very good job of saying so in the First Amendment. An early draft of the amendment read in part: "The civil rights of none shall be abridged on account of religious belief or worship, nor shall any national religion be established...." This draft was passed over. And, the founders had ample opportunity to state that the government should be allowed to promote all religion on an even-handed, non-preferential basis. But the Congress repeatedly rejected versions of the First Amendment that would have explicitly permitted such non-preferential aid. For example, the Senate rejected this proposed language: "Congress shall make no law establishing one religious sect or society in preference to others ...." And they rejected two more proposals with provisions embodying similar language, such as "Congress shall make no law establishing any particular denomination of religion in preference to another."[8]

No, the founders approved much more expansive language to keep the new federal government from making laws even "respecting an establishment of religion." Religion generally, not *a* religion or *a national* religion, but no religion at all. Period. They did not merely want to keep the federal government from setting up an official national church or to ban denominational discrimination.

In addition to constitutional history, there are practical reasons to reject the attempts of government to aid all religion on a non-preferential basis. In our pluralistic country with its amazing diversity, it would be impossible to aid all religions evenhandedly. Inevitably, government will pick and choose a preferred religion, and it almost always will select the majority, politically powerful, religious tradition for preferred treatment.

At the same time, a robust free exercise clause was intended to advance, or was at least consistent with, the notion that sometimes our religious practice must enjoy an exemption from generally applicable laws that apply to everyone else. By the time the First

Amendment was crafted, almost every state—with the exception of Connecticut—had a state constitutional provision protecting the free exercise of religion. Those provisions in state constitutions generally protected not only belief, but also actions based on those beliefs; the *exercise* of religion, not just the cause of conscience.

These protections could be compromised by the state only in those rare circumstances where "peace and safety," as well as "civil injury or outward disturbance of others" or in some cases "licentiousness or immorality," would result from the exercise of religion. In short, according to professor McConnell, "Both the affirmative free exercise protections and the peace and safety limitations flow logically from the liberal and evangelical theories of government" and provide a foreshadowing of the robust protections afforded by religious liberty in the Free Exercise Clause of the First Amendment.[9]

And, actual free exercise controversies in the pre-Constitution period often resulted in exemptions for religious scruples. These had to do with refusal to take oaths before giving testimony in court (Quakers and others), opposition to military conscription (Quakers/ Mennonites), objections to assessments and compelled tithes (Baptists/Quakers), and other issues such as refusal to remove one's hat in court as a sign of obeisance to civil authorities.[10]

It is true that these exemptions were granted by the legislatures and not the courts, but it is reasonable to assume that the legislatures granted the exemptions because they believed that the free exercise principle required them—not just because they were good policy. This view translates nicely, in an age of judicial review today, to a principle that would allow the courts to grant similar exemptions as a matter of constitutional entitlement.

The historical record argues persuasively that we have inherited constitutional constructs that were intended to provide strong protections for religious liberty.

In the next lecture, I want to flesh out what it means today to protect religious liberty and try to trace the Establishment Clause limits to free exercise accommodation. How do we handle the tension sometimes created by these two clauses to maximize religious liberty for all?

NOTES

[1]Walter B. Shurden, *The Baptist Identity: Four Fragile Freedoms* (Macon, GA: Smyth & Helwys, 1998), 49.

[2]Richard Groves, ed., *Thomas Helwys, A Short Declaration of the Mystery of Iniquity* (Macon, GA: Smyth & Helwys, 1998), preface.

[3]Roger Williams, "Mr. Cotton's Letter Lately Printed, Examined and Answered," in *The Complete Writings of Roger Williams*, vol. 1, ed. Perry Miller (New York: Russell and Russell, Inc., 1963), 108.

[4]John Clarke, "Ill News from New England," in *Colonial Baptists: Massachusetts and Rhode Island*, ed. Edwin S. Gaustad (New York: Arno Press, 1980), 51.

[5]*Isaac Backus on Church, State, and Calvinism*, Pamphlets 1754-1789 (William McLoughlin, ed., 1968).

[6]William R. Estep, *Revolution within the Revolution: The First Amendment in Historical Context, 1612-1789* (Grand Rapids: Eerdmans, 1990).

[7]Michael W. McConnell, "The Origins and Historical Understanding of Free Exercise of Religion," *Harvard Law Review* 103, no. 7 (May 1990): 1442-43.

[8]Douglas Laycock, "Nonpreferential Aid to Religion," *William and Mary Law Review* 27, no. 875 (1986): 879.

[9]McConnell, 1466.

[10]Ibid., 1467-68.

Lecture 2

First Freedom:
Accommodate Religion, But Don't Advance It

In the first lecture we discussed what I called "first principles" (theological and historical precedents). Now I want to talk about our first freedom: religious liberty—gifted by God but protected by our constitutional institutions, specifically the two religion clauses in the First Amendment, and how the two clauses operate together to ensure religious liberty.

Yes, religious liberty is the "first freedom" for the additional reason that the words protecting it in the First Amendment appear first in the Bill of Rights. The first sixteen words contain a clause preventing the establishment of religion and one to forbid interfering with the exercise of religion. It is not only listed before the others (press, speech, petition, and assembly), but the protection for religious liberty merits two clauses, not one. Both are equally important and must be taken seriously and be rigorously enforced if we are to adequately protect our religious liberty.

I want to make two general observations that will pervade our thinking today.

First, religious freedom in America is threatened by a wrong-headed belief among many that religious disputes should be settled by a majority vote. Although majoritarian principles are fundamental in a democracy—that's how we settle most political and policy issues—the Bill of Rights generally and the First Amendment's religion clauses in particular are "counter-majoritarian." They ensure the rights of minorities and protect against political majorities. They depend on the outcome of no election. The democratic majority sometimes can be as tyrannical as a totalitarian dictator. It is important to understand, as Justice Sandra Day O'Connor wrote in the Kentucky Ten Commandments case, one of her final opinions before retiring: "[W]e do not count heads before enforcing the First Amendment."[1] This counter-majoritarian understanding of the protections for religious freedom requires a robust enforcement of both religion clauses. If either clause is collapsed into the other or if both are watered down into a muddle of majoritarianism, religious liberty suffers.

Second, the majoritarian attitude that Justice O'Connor rejects is directly related to the deceptive notion of religious equality. Now to be sure, all religions should be treated equally, one with another. But when government treats religion the same as secular pursuits, we get into trouble. Religious liberty is often best ensured when government treats religion differently—sometimes extending religion special concessions and sometimes imposing on religion unique constraints.

Religion and religious institutions often are given certain concessions to lift burdens on the free exercise of religion. For example, a Baptist church is allowed to hire a Baptist music director instead of a Buddhist; for-profit businesses cannot discriminate on the basis of religion in hiring. Corporate lobbyists on K Street in Washington, D.C., must register under a lobby disclosure law; religious lobbies on Capitol Hill are exempt. Secular nonprofits, such as the United Way, are required to file a Form 990 disclosing information about their operation; religious nonprofits are generally relieved from this burdensome requirement. Houses of worship are exempt from having to install ramps and elevators under the Americans with Disabilities Act; secular public accommodations, such as a Holiday Inn, must comply. There are hundreds of other such examples where religious institutions should be and often are given special concessions to facilitate the free exercise of religion.

On the other hand, sometimes religion must endure special constraints to prevent the establishment of religion or to ensure compliance with Establishment Clause values. For example, public school teachers can say the Pledge of Allegiance, recite the Gettysburg Address, and voice many other things in a classroom, but they may not lead prayer or preside over religious exercises. Governmental buildings can display a portrait of the president of the United States, but they may not display a picture of Jesus or the

Christian cross. Government may fund many things, including the public schools, but it should not directly fund religion or religious schools. These limitations on religion operate to ensure government neutrality and promote religious liberty for all, especially religious minorities.

Unfortunately, the present trend is to defer to the will of political majorities, even where rights protected by the Bill of Rights are implicated, and to treat religion the same as secular pursuits. That attitude is precisely what informed the Supreme Court's disastrous 1990 opinion in *Employment Division v. Smith*,[2] the Native American peyote case. The Court's majority held that religious claims would not be entitled to exemptions from neutral, generally applicable laws. Religion should be treated no differently than secular counterparts. Five members of the Court concluded that this is simply an "unavoidable consequence of democratic government."[3] In effect, the Court told disappointed claimants to take their case to the legislative branch—the quintessential majoritarian political institution.

The Court has slowly chipped away at this principle of requiring constraints, especially regarding governmental funding of religion. For example, the Court has upheld the furnishing of computers and other educational equipment to church schools.[4] And, under certain circumstances, it has approved the use of school vouchers to support religious education.[5] Again, the attitude that has accompanied this march down the primrose path of government-funded religion is the misguided notion that religion should be treated the same as, or equal to, other pursuits.

This majoritarian idea of religious equality demeans religion at every turn and undermines religious freedom. When one "levels the playing field" for religion, as former BJC General Counsel Melissa Rogers is fond of saying, no one should be surprised when religion gets "leveled." Religion is special and different. Treating it as such best preserves religious liberty.

I want to begin with some basics. Both of the First Amendment's religion clauses—no establishment and free exercise—are essential to ensuring religious liberty. They stand as equal and counterpoising buttresses upholding the wall of separation between church and state, as the means to the end of ensuring religious liberty for all. A proper understanding of the institutional and functional separation of church and state, therefore, requires government to facilitate religion, but without advancing it; protect religion, but without promoting it; lift burdens on the exercise of religion, but without extending impermissible benefits.

Let's take free exercise first. Again, we have talked about the wisdom and sometimes the necessity of granting concessions or exemptions to laws that apply to everyone else in order to facilitate the exercise of religion. These religious exemptions generally fall into one of three categories: (1) mandatory, (2) permissible, and (3) impermissible.

Accommodations may be mandated when government has placed a substantial burden on the exercise of religion. These are usually required by the courts where the burden violates the Free Exercise Clause or overarching religious liberty statutes such as the Religious Freedom Restoration Act intended to re-create by statute the constitutional standard. Government can avoid this obligation only if it can show that it has a compelling governmental interest that it is pursuing in the least restrictive manner. Examples of these mandatory exemptions are demonstrated in Supreme Court cases involving excusal of Amish children from compulsory education laws, giving a Seventh-day Adventist unemployment compensation benefits while refusing to work on the Sabbath, and affording Santerias in South Florida the right to engage in animal sacrifice in their worship. All of this to say, where government regulation would violate one's free exercise rights, the courts—and sometimes legislatures—generally must provide an exemption to remove that burden absent a compelling public interest to the contrary. A really good reason.

Other cases involve situations where accommodation may not be required, but, for policy reasons, legislatures may decide to exempt religion anyway. These permissible accommodations will lift some governmental impediments to religious practice, even though they may not be substantial enough to trigger constitutional rights. Examples of this kind of accommodation are seen throughout federal and state law. They include exemption from taxation and various other tax breaks such as the ministerial housing allowance, an exemption from annual reporting requirements, a presumption of tax-exempt status for churches, and special protection against *invasive* governmental audits. Another example is the exemption in the Civil Rights Act of 1964 to allow religious organizations to discriminate on the basis of religion in hiring, even with respect to non-ministerial personnel. Religious organizations are often exempted from the nettlesome land-use regulations and zoning laws that impede a religious organization's ability to discharge its ministry and community service. Finally, the Supreme Court has ruled that states may provide financial aid for ministerial students in college or seminary, even though they are not constitutionally required to make such aid available. (Law professor Douglas Laycock discovered in 1992 some 2,000 religious exemptions in state and federal statutes—most of them permissible accommodations.)[6]

Sometimes an accommodation is neither mandated nor permitted. These involve ones that actually advance religion rather than accommodating it, promote religion rather than protecting it, provide a palpable benefit rather than lifting a burden. They often therefore violate the Establishment Clause. For example, a Connecticut law that required employers to grant leave to workers upon request for religious observance went too far and violated the Establishment Clause in large measure because that law would prejudice the employer and burden the rights of other employees who were not seeking accommodation.[7] The Court also has struck down attempts on the part of states to exempt religious periodicals from sales tax, because they were deemed an indirect subsidy and elevated religious speech to a higher level than comparable secular speech.[8]

The most controversial free exercise issue involving an exemption or an accommodation these days has to do with the Affordable Care Act (the new health care law) and contraception. That law requires employers with at least fifty employees to provide insurance coverage, including contraception for female employees who desire to obtain it. The law initially exempted churches and other houses of worship with conscience-based objections to contraception. It did not exempt religiously affiliated employers such as Catholic hospitals, colleges, and social service charities.

Many religious liberty advocates, including the Baptist Joint Committee, criticized the administration's failure to offer broader accommodation. Later, to its credit, the administration announced a modified policy that sought to strike a balance between the conscience rights of religiously affiliated employers who object to forms of contraception and the public interest of ensuring all women have access to preventative health care. Under the revised rules, objecting employers will not be required to offer or pay for employees' health care plans to cover contraception, but insurance providers must make such coverage available to all employees whose employers choose not to provide it. And a one-year safe harbor provision is currently in effect exempting religiously affiliated employers with objections to contraception coverage from complying.

In February 2013, the Obama administration also announced additional rules to clarify and expand the definition of "religious employer" and to detail the process by which self-insured employers would be required to allow a third party administrator to work with health insurers to extend that coverage, providing some distance between the employer and the employee desirous of contraception coverage.

The Baptist Joint Committee has taken the position that these accommodations are certainly permissible and perhaps required, and they were a politically reasonable effort seeking to balance the rights of employees who desire coverage. Many religious affiliates —including some Baptist colleges and agencies—have sued, claiming these accommodations are insufficient. These cases are working their way through the courts.

In addition to the accommodation for churches and religious affiliates, some seek to go even further. Some owners of for-profit, commercial businesses, often doing business as corporations, have taken the position that they too should be accorded an exemption, on equal footing with religiously affiliated nonprofits. Here, too, litigation has broken out in various jurisdictions, and I think that the U.S. Supreme Court will eventually have to decide this issue.

As a general proposition, individuals should not have to choose between their conscience and their chosen profession or business activity. The Free Exercise Clause and various federal statutes (such as the Religious Freedom Restoration Act and Title VII of the Civil Rights Act of 1964) can sometimes be asserted to obtain an accommodation even in an otherwise secular setting. However, the argument here against extending accommodation to for-profit, commercial enterprises is that any burden visited on the conscience of owners is at best remote and tenuous and not "substantial" as required for relief under the Constitution or federal law. Having to pay premiums to an insurance company that will then cover a full range of medical services, with the employee (who was hired without regard to religion) making her own independent determination about whether to use contraception, is arguably too attenuated a connection to substantially burden the owner's exercise of religion.

This law and this issue highlight an important concept. Many accommodations of religion—whether permissible or mandatory—visit no harm whatsoever on third parties. These include, for example, exempting members of the Native American church from laws banning the use of peyote, allowing the Amish, as we have said, to be exempt from compulsory education laws, excusing some religious groups (Hmongs, for example) from participating in autopsies otherwise required by law, and so forth. These are the easy accommodations to make. Far more difficult are cases where, as with the Affordable Care Act, the rights and well-being of third parties are directly affected by the requested accommodation. These have often been denied as the courts try to balance free exercise rights of the claimant with the rights of those detrimentally affected. Even if there is a substantial burden in the first place, courts may find that government has a compelling interest in protecting the welfare of those third parties and, sometimes, would rule the accommodation actually violates the Establishment Clause.

Now, let me talk briefly about the Establishment Clause. Again, as we have said, the Free Exercise Clause sometimes requires certain concessions to be made to religion; the Establishment Clause sometimes requires certain constraints to be imposed on religion for government to maintain its neutrality and to adequately ensure religious liberty. If the Free Exercise Clause keeps government from hurting religion (and sometimes requires an accommodation), the Establishment Clause keeps government from trying to help religion. Changing the metaphor slightly, Dean Kelley, the great Methodist pastor and religious liberty advocate of a generation ago, often observed, "Government may and sometimes must get out of the way of religion, but it should never, ever get behind and push."

In the first lecture, we talked about what I think our nation's founders meant by the Establishment Clause. Let me briefly sketch out what the thinking is today.

Some people take a narrow or weak view of the Establishment Clause. People in this camp say that government cannot coerce religious choices—requiring you to do something your religion forbids or preventing you from doing something your religion requires. They understand the language of the First Amendment only to prevent government from preferring one religion over another or from setting up an official state church. But they would allow government to aid or promote religion generally and evenhandedly.

Others, including the Baptist Joint Committee and myself, take what is often referred to as a broad or strong view of the "no establishment" clause. As I argued in the first lecture, it sees the language of the First Amendment to prevent government endorsement of and aid to religion in general—not just as a ban on denominational discrimination, outright coercion, or setting up an official state religion. One of the most compelling arguments behind this view is that our founders considered and rejected several proposed amendments that would have expressly allowed government to advance religion generally, even if it did not favor one religion over another.

This strong view has generally been the one that has prevailed in the U.S. Supreme Court. In fact, in the first modern Establishment Clause case decided after World War II, all nine justices embraced this broad view of the Establishment Clause.[9] Today,

I am distressed to report that the Court is pretty evenly divided, four or five taking the narrow view and four or five taking the broad view, depending upon the case.

Establishment Clause cases tend to fall into one of two general areas. First, concerns are raised when government expresses an official opinion on or takes sides in matters of religion. It has to do with attempts by government to promote or endorse religion in words or symbols. These cases involve, for example, government displays of the Ten Commandments, state-approved prayer and religious exercises in the public schools, or government-sponsored displays of crèches and other religious symbols.

The second general category of Establishment Clause cases has to do, not with what government says or endorses, but with what it does with its checkbook. These are funding cases involving claims that the government establishes religion by supporting religious organizations, programs, or enterprises with tax dollars. Examples of this include attempts by government to subsidize religious ministries through the so-called faith-based initiative and efforts to subsidize religious education, as was attempted in Florida in the fall of 2012 through the failed effort to repeal the "no-aid" provision of the Florida state constitution.

Now, I want to conclude with a short discussion of a third area of church-state jurisprudence that issues from both the Establishment Clause and the Free Exercise Clause. It is called the church autonomy doctrine.

Basically, it says that government, particularly the courts, must defer to religious organizations to make their own decisions about matters of doctrine, internal governance, polity, and administration. This rule of judicial deference typically comes up in cases arising out of employment disputes within religious organizations and property ownership issues surrounding church splits. This doctrine also means that courts are supposed to define "religion" expansively and generously and are absolutely barred from judging the truth, validity, reasonableness, consistency, or orthodoxy of beliefs.

This is an important part of U.S. law that protects the integrity and autonomy of religious bodies. A case in the U.S. Supreme Court in 2012 dealt with this principle.[10]

In this landmark decision, the High Court upheld the so-called "ministerial exception"—a specific application of the church autonomy doctrine that prohibits courts from intervening in employment discrimination disputes between churches and their ordained ministers. When dealing with the local church and its ministers, this rule is pretty clear-cut and makes a lot of sense. Far more problematic in this case was the fact that it dealt with a religious school—not a local church—and with a teacher who had both secular and religious duties at the school. In addition to secular subjects, the "commissioned" (similar to ordained) teacher taught a religion class, led her students in daily prayer and devotional exercises, and participated in school-wide chapel services.

The Court, in a unanimous opinion, held that the teacher was a ministerial employee based on the circumstances of her employment and, as such, she could not file a discrimination suit against the school when it fired her for reasons that might have otherwise violated the Americans with Disabilities Act. Writing for the Court, Chief Justice John Roberts observed that "the interest of society in the enforcement of employment discrimination statutes is undoubtedly important. But so too is the interest of religious groups in choosing who will preach their beliefs, teach their faith, and carry out their mission." Chief Justice Roberts concluded that "the church must be free to choose those who will guide it on its way."[11]

The church autonomy doctrine is important. When it applies, there is no balancing as with free exercise cases. Keeping courts from making decisions about theological and ecclesiological matters is crucial to protecting religious liberty.

I began this lecture by talking about the counter-majoritarian nature of the two religion clauses and their protection for religious freedom. I want to conclude by giving somewhat of an ironic twist to that assertion. For this counter-majoritarian understanding of the First Amendment's religion clauses to survive over time, it must be embraced by a majority, if not a consensus, of the American people—not just by judges, activists, and academics. After all, counter-majoritarian constitutional provisions can be changed by a super-majority if they can get enough votes.

I think popular acceptance of the counter-majoritarian principle and the vision for a robust application of the religion clauses can be encouraged through appeals to a sense of fundamental fairness and common courtesy. I have often propounded something that would do us a lot of good. It's akin to the Golden Rule. We might even call it a golden rule for church-state relations. This is something we all should be able to rally around, believers and nonbelievers alike, from left to right on the political spectrum. My golden rule for church and state would go like this: "I cannot ask government to promote my religion if I don't want government to promote somebody else's religion; and I cannot permit government to hinder somebody else's religion if I don't want government to hinder my religion."

If appeals to constitutional principles and fundamental fairness do not do the trick, then maybe an appeal to enlightened self-interest will. Patently reasonable application of the religion clauses would support a regime where a government protects all religion and promotes none—ensuring religious freedom for all for years to come. Accommodating religion, yes; but advancing religion, no!

NOTES

[1] *McCreary County v. ACLU of Kentucky*, 545 U.S. 844, 884 (2005) (O'Connor, concurring).

[2] *Employment Division v. Smith*, 494 U.S. 872 (1990).

[3] Ibid., 890.

[4] *Mitchell v. Helms*, 530 U.S. 793 (2000).

[5] *Zelman v. Simmons-Harris*, 536 U.S. 639 (2002).

[6] Douglas Laycock, "Regulatory Exemptions of Religious Behavior and the Original Understanding of the Establishment Clause," *Notre Dame Law Review* 81 (2006): 1793, 1837.

[7] *Estate of Thornton v. Caldor, Inc.,* 472 U.S. 703 (1985).

[8] *Texas Monthly, Inc. v. Bullock*, 489 U.S. 1 (1989).

[9] *Everson v. Board of Education*, 330 U.S. 1 (1947).

[10] *Hosanna-Tabor Evangelical Church and School v. EEOC*, 132 S.Ct. 694 (2012).

[11] Ibid., 710.

Lecture 3

Religion and Politics:
How Did We Do in 2012?

The separation of church and state—as important as it is—does not require a complete segregation of religion from politics or strip the public square of religious discourse. People of faith have the same right as anyone else to seek to vend their views in the marketplace of ideas and—with some limits—to convert their religious ethics into public policy by organizing, speaking out, voting, and running for and serving in office. The metaphorical wall of separation does not block metaphysical assumptions from influencing public life.

People of faith need not limit their piety to the church house or to acts of private devotion, nor must they concede the public square to others. They should be involved and seek to transform our culture in part through the political process.

The question is not whether religious people will be involved in politics, but how they should do it. People of faith and Baptists in particular—unlike our Anabaptist cousins—have always been involved in public life.

Yes, people of faith today can "occupy Wall Street" or have a "tea party."

So my thesis is that a conversation about religion—and religion itself—can be a positive force in politics, not only in lobbying for reform, but also when running for and serving in office.

When candidates talk about their faith, it can help us know who they are, learn what makes them tick, and examine their moral core. The free and fluid discussion of candidates' faith carries the promise of improving the electorate's ability to make an informed decision in the voting booth.

All of that said, we must keep several things in mind. Danger always lurks when we try to combine religion and politics—two things, it is said, you do not want to discuss in polite company. I want to mention two overarching limitations and set out three specific caveats or words of caution to guide our thinking and behavior about how we put those two things together: religion and politics.

First, Article VI of the U.S. Constitution bans religious tests for public office. Most of the American colonies had a variety of religious tests for public office, but the wise architects of our republic had a different vision in mind. They would tolerate no religious tests for the new federal government. Although that provision technically only bans legal disabilities for qualifications for office and constrains only the government, we (the electorate) should make every effort, as good citizens, to live up to the *spirit* as well as the letter of Article VI. Religion may be a part of the mix, but we should not impose a religious litmus test.

This means that a discussion of candidates' religion ought to be permissible but never mandatory. We should respect candidates' preference not to bear their religious convictions in public, if they choose not to do so, as long as they are fully forthcoming in explaining their position on policy issues and how they arrived at them (for example, Bill Bradley, John Kerry, Howard Dean, Rudy Giuliani, John McCain, Mitt Romney).

How about non-believers—atheists, agnostics, secularists, those who are "religiously unaffiliated" (collectively 19 percent of the population)? They should not be prejudiced in the political arena. Openly professed atheism is perhaps the most significant electoral liability in American political culture. The most religious candidate is not necessarily the best qualified leader of our secular, religiously plural country and culture. As Martin Luther once said, better to be ruled by a smart Turk than a dumb Christian. Billy Graham, of all people, has said, "Religious conviction alone was not the most reliable guide as to who would be the best or most effective leader."[1] The "no religious test" clause should be a guiding principle that goes beyond formal legal qualifications.

Second, when religion is discussed, it is essential to ask about how candidates' religious views will impact public policy positions and leadership competence. It is always important to ask the "what difference will it make" question. It is not only not very helpful but also terribly invasive to have a theological inquiry isolated from policy and matters of governance.

So, along with any discussion of a candidate's faith, we must always ask the follow-up "so what" question: What difference will a theological position make on the candidate's ability to be president or vice president? Let us think about a few examples.

A devout and observant orthodox Jew ran for vice president in the year 2000. It was quite appropriate to inquire of Senator Joe Lieberman what would happen if a national emergency occurred on his Sabbath. Would he be able to perform his duties of office despite the restrictions on his activity that day of the week?

What if a Quaker, Mennonite, or someone from a peace denominational background were to run for president? It would be entirely appropriate to inquire about how his or her pacifism would affect defense policy. If elected, could the candidate use force of arms to defend the country?

How about conservative Protestants? Might their eschatology or view of the end times affect their foreign policy views, particularly with regard to the Middle East?

How about a Catholic candidate or a Mormon? What happens when the Pope or a member of the First Presidency issues an edict that contravenes their duty of office? Of course we had this issue with JFK in 1960 and Mitt Romney the past two election cycles.

What I'm talking about actually happened during the vice presidential debates in 2012. You may remember that Martha Raddatz asked Vice President Joe Biden and Rep. Paul Ryan, both observant Catholics, about their position on abortion and how their Catholic beliefs impacted that decision. This was an entirely appropriate question to ask.

A blatant breach of this principle was when Rev. Robert Jeffress openly dismissed Governor Romney's candidacy simply because he is a Mormon without drawing any connection to his fitness for office. Actually, that may not be the most blatant example.

On a trip to Texas in the fall of 2012, I saw—and it was on Facebook and the Internet as well—a sign at a church saying,

"Vote for the Mormon, not the Muslim! The capitalist, not the communist!" It goes without saying that, in addition to needing to draw a tight fit between religious belief and an issue that matters, you should not lie.

In addition to the "no religious test" principle and the importance of asking the "so what" follow-up question, I want to offer three words of caution, or caveats, to the general proposition that religion can be helpful and should be a part of our public discourse.

The first is *theological* in nature. Any foray into politics with focused religious motivation should be tempered with a dose of humility, for good reason. Was it Blaise Pascal who said that "men never do evil so completely and cheerfully as when they do it from religious conviction"? We need to understand that, however sure we think we are of our position, the other person at least has something to say and maybe, in the final analysis, is right. As my predecessor James Dunn has said of the bombastic broadsides that we've heard mainly from the religious right in recent years, "What they say is not totally false; it is falsely total." It lacks a note of self-evaluation, of tentativeness, of nuance, of humility that one needs to bring to bear on a public policy message based squarely on one's religious conviction. This goes for extremism on the religious left, too.

Barbara Jordan, our Baptist sister, had it right. At a meeting of the Baptist Joint Committee some twenty-five years ago, she was asked how to properly articulate Christian values in government. Her response went something like this: "You would do well to pursue your causes with vigor, while remembering that you are a servant of God, not a spokesperson for God, and remembering that God may choose to bless an opposing point of view for reasons that have not been revealed to you." The theological principle or caveat of humility must come into play to temper our religious exuberance.

The second caveat is *ethical* in nature. It has to do with the use or abuse of "civil religion"—that blending of a generic Judeo-Christian piety with American patriotism to the point that one cannot tell them apart. It should not surprise us that, in a country as outwardly religious as the U.S., references to God will pop up in our civil ceremonies, mottos, slogans, and public rituals. These include "under God" in the Pledge of Allegiance, "In God We Trust" on coins, and the ubiquitous "God Bless America" at the end of almost every speech of public officials. This is sometimes referred to as "ceremonial deism."

These acknowledgements of our religious heritage generally have been tolerated by our courts. But, I bristle when it seems civil religion is used to advance a political agenda—by voters, pundits, and political parties, as well as public officials. I would urge that we apply some prudential breaks here—some self-restraint—on the general idea that talking about religion in public life is—or can be—a benefit. It is always dicey and difficult to judge a politician's sincerity and good faith. I guess we do it the same way we make other judgments about such matters: observing the demeanor of the speaker and seeking to determine if they "walk the walk" as well as "talk the talk." As a matter of ethics, responsible speech, and prudent behavior, we need to be careful about permitting religion to be the handmaiden of political expediency.

The third cautionary note is *legal and constitutional* in nature. For starters, we have legal issues dealing with electioneering activities on the part of churches and other nonprofits exempt from taxation under section 501(c)(3). In exchange for this most favorable tax status (where the entity is tax-exempt and donations are deductible), these nonprofits are deemed to have agreed not to use their funds to endorse or oppose candidates for office. We do not finance political campaigns with before-tax dollars.

Under this provision of the tax code, churches and other nonprofits, of course, can engage fully and freely in issue advocacy. This is a part of their prophetic function, and houses of worship can speak out on the great moral issues of the day from the pulpit, through publications, and in other ways. Similarly, these nonprofits can engage in some "lobbying" activities—attempting to influence legislation in Congress, state legislatures, and other legislative fora.

However, electioneering—supporting or opposing candidates for office—is completely banned. So the watch words are: Issues, yes! Candidates, no!

So churches cannot endorse candidates, make donations to candidates' campaigns, engage in fundraising activities on behalf of candidates, distribute statements supporting or opposing a candidate, or issue partisan statements from the pulpit, on stationery, or in official publications and websites.

That said, there is still a lot that churches can do. These have to do with education and good citizenship initiatives that are nonpartisan in nature. These include such things as sponsoring debates on issues, inviting candidates to speak (if all candidates are invited), teaching the importance of good citizenship, encouraging people to vote, registering people to vote, and distributing nonpartisan and unbiased information on issues and candidates' voting records. And, of course, ministers and church leaders *individually* may support (even publicly) any candidate they wish, as long as it is outside of their official role as representative of the nonprofit entity.

As you know, there are gray areas here. Where does issue advocacy bleed over into endorsement of the candidate? What happens if you preach on a defining issue the Sunday before the election and, because of how the issue is spoken of, a reasonable observer could infer that you're endorsing a candidate? How about allowing a candidate to address the congregation even if it's not a political speech? The IRS has issued some good guidelines that help with many of these close issues. And those guidelines can be accessed on their website.

We have had some efforts over the past several years—misguided in my view—in Congress to pass a law that would allow churches—but not secular nonprofits—to endorse candidates from the pulpit with impunity and without jeopardizing tax-exempt status. More recent efforts are not limited to religious bodies. This kind of legal permission to blend churches and partisan politics—even more than they already are—is a bad idea because it would be highly divisive and terribly corrosive, and it would politicize churches far more than it would Christianize parties. It would also have the effect of turning our pulpit prophets into political puppets.

So far, we have talked about the electioneering phase. There are constitutional issues surrounding the governing phase of public life. The ultimate outcome of religiously motivated policy initiatives should always have a secular purpose and have the primary effect that does not advance religion. That's what Rep. David Price, D-N.C., means when he talks about "a coincidence of the religious precept with broader public values," advancing common good, not just a narrow sectarian agenda. For example, Alabama Supreme Court Chief Justice Roy Moore clearly crossed the line when he installed the two-ton monolith bearing the Ten Commandments, as every court that looked at the case concluded. But, at the same time, Alabama Gov. Bob Riley was seeking tax reform, explicitly citing his Christian beliefs for justification. Riley's religious motivation, however, I submit was proper because there were a number of non-religious arguments and secular justifications to support tax reform.

Think of it this way: there are many ways to say it. Religion plays an important, but limited, role. While it is permissible for religion to motivate a policy, it should not dominate it. Jon Meacham, author of the book *American Gospel*, has said religion is a thread in the tapestry of American life, not the tapestry itself. In the book, he says religion should shape policy, but not strangle it. Moreover, if the only rationale for a policy position is an *a priori* religious assertion, it is hard for it to be debated and tested in the marketplace of ideas and on the political scene. There should be a broader non-religious rationale articulated for public policy that is based on faith conviction. Otherwise, it runs the risk of violating the First Amendment's ban on the establishment of religion.

So, I don't want us to shy away from talking about separation of church and state as some are wont to do these days. Properly understood, it does not ban, but in a sense makes possible, the free discussion of religion and religious themes in the public square. And with the "no religious test" principle in mind and the "so what" question constantly on our lips, and with the three caveats I have mentioned—theological, ethical, and legal/constitutional—I think a robust conversation in the public square is good for religion and good for the body politic.

Now, looking specifically at the 2012 elections, for all of the talk among evangelical Christians and others that they would never vote for a Mormon, there is no evidence to suggest that Governor Romney's defeat was related to his Mormonism. True, there may be some who refused to vote for him because of his religion and others who did not vote at all for that reason, but President Obama's margin of victory far exceeded any disability suffered by Governor Romney because of his religion. We also can take some satisfaction in knowing that the Democratic Party, along with sympathetic political action committees, did not raise Governor Romney's Mormonism as an issue that was at all relevant to the election.

It also seems we did a pretty good job of talking about religion in the public square in a responsible way. With rare exception, we did a commendable job in balancing the pertinence of religion to public life with the prohibition on religious tests.

In addition to the unprecedented religious makeup of both presidential tickets (no White Anglo-Saxon Protestant) and the Supreme Court (first time in 225 years: no Protestants) and treating religion responsibly in the public square, the outcome in congressional races also gives cause for optimism.

Two Muslim members of the House of Representatives, Keith Ellison, D-Minn., and André Carson, D-Ind., were re-elected. After serving in the House, Mazie Hirono, D-Hawaii, became the first Buddhist ever to be elected to the Senate. Tulsi Gabbard, D-Hawaii, became the first Hindu to be elected to the House of Representatives. Finally, Kyrsten Sinema, D-Ariz., was elected to the House of Representatives as the only self-confessed "religiously unaffiliated" member. (Confessed atheist, Rep. Pete Stark, D-Calif., served twenty terms in Congress before losing his seat in 2012.)

Moreover, we appear to have come to terms with members of Congress who are neither Christian nor Jewish taking oaths of office on their own holy books. When Representative Ellison was first elected in 2007 and opted to take his oath of office on the Quran, a great outcry arose. Many insisted he use the Bible even though he is a Muslim. None of that appeared to happen in 2013. Representative Gabbard affirmed her oath on the Bhagavad Gita, the Hindu holy book; Senator Hirono opted against placing her hand on any book; and Representative Sinema chose, appropriately enough, to place her hand on a copy of the U.S. Constitution. Hardly a peep of protest could be heard in opposition to these conscientious practices of these members of Congress.

I recognize we continue to have a long way to go. Many still think that we are and should be a "Christian nation," legally and constitutionally, not just demographically. A recent Huffington Post/YouGov poll reveals 34 percent favor establishing Christianity as the official religion in their state. Islamophobia and anti-Mormon prejudice prevail in many quarters. However, the fact that an overwhelming Christian majority is willing to elect legislators who reflect America's plush pluralism and astonishing religious diversity and give them permission to solemnize their investiture without protest suggests to me that we are making some progress.

May we continue to move forward in our thinking and practice. The "no religious test" principle in the Constitution must go hand in glove with the First Amendment's two religion clauses and church autonomy doctrine; they are equally important in protecting religious liberty in a nation whose religious tapestry is becoming increasingly variegated.

NOTE

[1]Billy Graham, *Just as I Am: The Autobiography of Billy Graham* (San Francisco: HarperSanFrancisco, 1997), 493.

Appendix

The First Amendment
to the United States Constitution

Congress shall make no law respecting an establishment of religion, or prohibiting the free exercise thereof; or abridging the freedom of speech, or of the press; or the right of the people peaceably to assemble, and to petition the Government for a redress of grievances.

Frequently Asked Questions about the Baptist Joint Committee for Religious Liberty

The BJC's mission is to defend and extend God-given religious liberty for all, furthering the Baptist heritage that champions the principle that religion must be freely exercised, neither advanced nor inhibited by government.

What is the Baptist Joint Committee for Religious Liberty?

The BJC is a nonpartisan, nonprofit 501(c)(3) education and advocacy denominational organization that defends religious freedom and upholds the principle of church-state separation. While primarily supported by Baptists (denominational groups, churches, and individuals), the BJC works for religious liberty for all, including Jewish, Muslim, and a host of Christian and minority religious groups that count on the organization for leadership.

The BJC is the only religious agency devoted solely to the principles of religious liberty outlined in the First Amendment, and it leads key coalitions of religious and civil liberties groups striving to protect both the free exercise of religion and to defend against its establishment by government.

Who supports the Baptist Joint Committee?

The BJC is supported by fifteen Baptist bodies in the United States and thousands of churches and individuals across the country. The BJC's board of directors is composed of representatives of the fifteen supporting Baptist organizations.

- Alliance of Baptists
- American Baptist Churches USA
- Baptist General Association of Virginia
- Baptist General Convention of Missouri (Churchnet)

- Baptist General Convention of Texas
- Converge Worldwide (BGC)
- Cooperative Baptist Fellowship
- Cooperative Baptist Fellowship of North Carolina
- National Baptist Convention of America
- National Baptist Convention USA Inc.
- National Missionary Baptist Convention
- North American Baptists Inc.
- Progressive National Baptist Convention Inc.
- Religious Liberty Council
- Seventh Day Baptist General Conference

What does the Baptist Joint Committee do?

The BJC promotes religious freedom through three major activities: legislation, litigation, and education.

Its legislative work includes monitoring legislation relating to church-state matters, and its efforts often are coordinated with coalitions of other groups. On any particular bill the BJC may analyze the legislation, join coalition efforts for or against the bill, lead congressional staff briefings on the need for or implications of a bill, or contact legislative offices directly on behalf of the BJC.

The organization also monitors church-state litigation, providing analysis of cases and participating in some of the more pressing matters affecting religious freedom. The BJC does not initiate litigation, but participates primarily through coordinated *amicus curiae* (friend-of-the-court) briefs at the U.S. Supreme Court and other courts. The BJC is often asked to join such efforts, as well as to contribute to the planning, writing, and editing process, or to do outreach for additional support for *amicus* efforts.

In addition, the BJC is involved in ongoing education efforts, developing resources and leading educational programs. The organization often hosts groups in its Center for Religious Liberty on Capitol Hill, and staff members routinely are quoted in the media and speak in locations across the country, including churches, universities, seminaries, and civic gatherings.

How does the Baptist Joint Committee help churches?

In addition to serving churches as a religious liberty watchdog agency in the nation's capital, the BJC staff often leads educational programs in churches, including preaching sermons and teaching Sunday school, and publishes resources on religious liberty issues for congregational use. The organization also can be counted on if church leaders have particular church-state questions about which they would like to consult.

Why does the Baptist Joint Committee support church-state separation?

The separation of church and state, or the "wall of separation" talked about by early Baptist Roger Williams, framer Thomas Jefferson, and the U.S. Supreme Court, is simply a shorthand metaphor for expressing a deeper truth. Religious liberty is best protected when church and state are institutionally separated and neither tries to perform or interfere with the essential mission and work of the other.

When government and religion are merged, one of two things happens, and both are bad. At worst, consciences are violated, leading sometimes to persecution. At the very least, state-controlled religion—even in the hands of a benevolent government—waters religion down and robs it of its vitality.

Is the Baptist Joint Committee non-partisan?

Yes. The mission of the Baptist Joint Committee is focused solely on advocating religious liberty and its constitutional corollary, the separation of church and state. The BJC does not support or oppose candidates for elective office. The BJC pursues a balanced, sensibly centrist position on church-state issues, affirming both religion clauses in the First Amendment—no establishment and free exercise—as essential to guaranteeing our God-given religious freedom.

Does the Baptist Joint Committee speak for Baptists?

The BJC does not claim to speak for all Baptists or for any Baptist on all issues. It speaks to Baptists and to others about what it means to be Baptist. In this sense, the BJC exists to serve Baptists by defending and extending freedom for all.

What is the history of the Baptist Joint Committee?

The BJC traces its roots to 1936 as the Southern Baptist Committee on Public Relations. After joining forces with American and National Baptists, the committee established offices in Washington, D.C., in 1946 and became the Baptist Joint Committee on Public Affairs. The BJC is now sponsored by all Baptist groups in the United States listed on pages 41 and 42. In 2005, the BJC name changed to the Baptist Joint Committee for Religious Liberty to more accurately reflect its singular focus on religious liberty issues.

How can I connect with the Baptist Joint Committee?

Visit the BJC's website at www.BJConline.org and read the blog at www.BJConline.org/blog to keep up with the latest news. You also can subscribe to the organization's email list and magazine, *Report from the Capital,* by sending your email and mailing address to bjc@BJConline.org. Plus, you can follow the BJC on Facebook at www.Facebook.com/ReligiousLiberty or Twitter @BJContheHill.

If you are visiting Washington, D.C., and would like to bring a group to the BJC's Center for Religious Liberty for an educational session, call the BJC at (202) 544-4226 or send an email to bjc@BJConline.org.

A Brief History
of the Shurden Lectures

In 2004, Walter B. Shurden and Kay W. Shurden of Macon, Georgia, made a gift to the Baptist Joint Committee to establish an annual lectureship on the issues of religious liberty and the separation of church and state. The lecturers may be academicians, politicians, ministers, church historians, ethicists, or activists. Above all, the Shurden lecturer is someone who can inspire and call others to an ardent commitment to religious freedom and the separation of church and state.

Designed to enhance the ministry and programs of the BJC, the lectures are held at Mercer University in Macon every three years and at another seminary, college, or university the other years.

A nationally noted church historian, Dr. Walter Shurden is the founding executive director of the Center for Baptist Studies and a minister at large for Mercer University. He served at Mercer for almost twenty-five years as Callaway Professor of Christianity in the Roberts Department of Christianity in the College of Liberal Arts. During eighteen of those years, he served as chair of the department.

Dr. Kay W. Shurden, a retired professor in the Department of Psychiatry and Behavioral Sciences at the Mercer University School of Medicine, is a noted author and maintains a private practice in counseling and supervision.

For more information on the lecture series—including a link to watch some of the previous presentations online—visit www.BJConline.org/lectures.

Previous Lecturers, Venues, and Lecture Titles

<u>2006</u>
Mercer University
Macon, Georgia

DAVID SAPERSTEIN
Director, Religious Action Center of Reform Judaism

"The Framers, the Justices, and Us:
    An Overview of Changing Church-State Relations in American Life"
"The Use and Abuse of Religion in American Political and Public Life:
    Elections, Ten Commandments, and Intelligent Design"
"Separation of Church and State in Israel:
    Insight from Another Democracy"

<u>2007</u>
Carson-Newman University
Jefferson City, Tennessee

JAMES M. DUNN
Professor of Christianity and Public Policy,
    Wake Forest Divinity School
Former executive director, Baptist Joint Committee for Religious Liberty

"Challenging Religion: Ours Is … We Are …"
"Response Able and Free"
"The Prophethood of All Believers"

2008
Wake Forest University Divinity School
Winston-Salem, North Carolina

CHARLES G. ADAMS
Pastor, Hartford Memorial Baptist Church, Detroit, Michigan

"Sermon as Song"
"Preserve Religious Liberty"
"All Things Are Yours"

2009
Mercer University
Macon, Georgia

RANDALL BALMER
Professor of religious history, Barnard College; author

"So Help Me God:
        Religion and the Presidency Since John F. Kennedy"
"Where Have All the Baptists Gone?
        The Betrayal of an American Institution"
"Keep the Faith:
        Reclaiming Christianity from the Religious Right"

2010
Samford University
Birmingham, Alabama

MARTIN E. MARTY
Former professor of religious history,
        University of Chicago; author

"On Not Privileging the Privileging of Religion:
        A Clue from Montesquieu"
"On the Difference Indifference Can Make:
        A Clue from Franklin"
"On Tracing Lines, Not Building Walls:
        A Clue from Madison"

<u>2011</u>
Georgetown College
Georgetown, Kentucky

MELISSA ROGERS
Director, Center for Religion and Public Affairs,
*   Wake Forest University Divinity School*
Senior fellow, Brookings Institution

"Religious Expression in American Public Life"
"An American and Christian Case for Defending Muslims' Free
       Exercise Rights"
"Faith-Based Partnerships under Presidents Bush and Obama"

<u>2012</u>
Mercer University
Macon, Georgia

FRANKLIN T. LAMBERT
Professor of history, Purdue University; author

"America Conceived as a Christian Nation?
       The Separation of Good and Bad History"
"A Secular/Sacred Alliance in the Fight for Religious Liberty"
"Constituting the Separation of Church and State"

<u>2013</u>
Stetson University
DeLand, Florida

BRENT WALKER
Executive director,
*   Baptist Joint Committee for Religious Liberty*

"First Principles:
       God-Given, But Government Protected"
"First Freedoms:
       Accommodate Religion, But Don't Advance It"
"Religion and Politics:
       How Did We Do in 2012?"

A Lunch That Launched
a Vital Lectureship

By J. Brent Walker

(This article is adapted from one published in the April 2013 edition of *Report from the Capital*, the magazine of the Baptist Joint Committee for Religious Liberty.)

O ur good friends, Buddy and Kay Shurden, invited me to come to Macon to have lunch with them in the fall of 2004. They said they had something they wanted to talk over with me. You cannot possibly imagine how hard my jaw hit the floor when, after a very nice lunch, they handed me a check for $100,000 to endow a lectureship on religious liberty and the separation of church and state. This was an astonishingly generous gift from two teachers on the cusp of retirement after rearing and educating three children and performing many acts of generosity toward their church and other charitable causes.

Their idea was for the Baptist Joint Committee to join with different colleges and seminaries once a year—with the lectures returning to Mercer University every third year—to inform and excite the next generation of students about the importance of these topics to both the kingdom of God and the kingdom of Caesar. They expressed to me an urgent desire to foster accurate and inspiring education about this topic for which they harbored a signal passion.

"We believe that the threat to religious liberty and the separation of church and state is epidemic in America today," they said. "This threat comes from the courthouse, the White House, and church house. No potatoes are hotter in public discourse than issues of church and state: vouchers, prayer in public schools, faith-based charities, and the places of the Ten Commandments. The BJC is the kitchen where those potatoes are being baked. We, therefore, believe that the BJC is one of the most crucial religious organizations in this republic."

Buoyed by their kind words and armed with wherewithal to match, the Walter B. and Kay W. Shurden Lectures on Religious Liberty and Separation of Church and State commenced eighteen months later in the spring of 2006, with Rabbi David Saperstein, director of the Religious Action Center of Reform Judaism, delivering the inaugural lectures at Mercer University in Macon, Georgia. In 2013, we concluded the eighth annual Shurden Lectures at Stetson University in DeLand, Florida. I was privileged to have the opportunity to deliver these at my law school alma mater.

In between Rabbi Saperstein and me, six others have helped advance the Shurdens' vision, delivering lectures at Carson-Newman University (James Dunn), Wake Forest University (Charles Adams), Samford University (Martin Marty), Georgetown College (Melissa Rogers), and Mercer University (Randall Balmer and Frank Lambert). The venues for the next three Shurden Lectures have been set: Baylor University (2014), Mercer University (2015), and Bethel University (2016).

These lectures have provided wonderful opportunities for thousands of students, professors, and other campus visitors to imbibe the wisdom the speakers supplied. All lectures delivered after 2008 are posted on the Baptist Joint Committee's Vimeo website in video form (Vimeo.com/bjcvideos), and more recent ones as podcasts on the BJC's iTunes channel for an untold number of learners to enjoy.

The Shurdens have always put their money where their hearts lie. After making their generous gift, they expressed their desire "to ignite renewed passion for historic Baptist ideas." They concluded, "We want our grandchildren and their children to live in an America where those values are not only preserved but also championed. Those values, we believe, make for a more vigorous religion and a healthier state."

With the opening of the new Center for Religious Liberty in October 2012, the BJC's opportunities for educating the next generation of religious liberty advocates have never been better.

During the six months after the Center's opening, the BJC staff has deliberately focused on crafting goals and priorities to fully employ the Center and the BJC's resources for our education efforts. We are eager to reach the audiences the Shurdens had in mind. As part of this, the BJC will hire a new, full-time education and outreach specialist to implement a strategy to accomplish our goals. This is a major investment for the BJC, and we hope to fill the position by mid-summer.

Just as the Shurden Lectures would not be possible without Buddy and Kay's vision and financial commitment, we cannot fund the education and outreach specialist position and the programs that person will implement without your support. Your gift of any amount will help us fund these new initiatives. Won't you join the Shurdens in this effort to help the BJC defend and extend religious liberty by teaching others how to join in this fight? Can you imagine a more worthy legacy to leave?

(In July 2013, the BJC hired Charles Watson Jr. as the education and outreach specialist.)

Clearing up Misconceptions at the Church-State Intersection

By Jeff Huett

(This article is adapted from one published in the April 2013 edition of *Report from the Capital*, the magazine of the Baptist Joint Committee for Religious Liberty.)

In a September 1992 comic strip, the precocious 6-year-old half of *Calvin and Hobbes* called the separation of church and state a "touchy subject." Over the course of three presentations at Stetson University April 9-10, Baptist Joint Committee Executive Director Brent Walker drew on this description, presenting some of the misunderstandings that make religious liberty and church-state separation controversial and suggesting ways to accommodate religious differences, even in the political realm.

Walker was the speaker for the BJC's eighth annual Walter B. and Kay W. Shurden Lectures on Religious Liberty and Separation of Church and State. In 2004, the Shurdens of Macon, Georgia, made a gift to the BJC to establish the annual lectureship, held annually on college campuses.

Walker explained that issues at the intersection of church and state "go to matters of the heart, to our faith in God, and the dizzying diversity of religious expression we find in this country."

In his first lecture, Walker laid the foundation for the proper relationship between church and state with respect to theology and history. "Religious liberty is a gift from God, not the result of any act of toleration on the part of government," he said. God is seen as a "liberating deity" in Scripture "who loves his children and cares about that relationship enough to create us free to say 'no,'" Walker said.

Walker then discussed the role of Baptists in championing religious liberty and church-state separation. From their reliance on Scripture to suffering the hard lessons of persecution, Baptists' understanding of religious freedom "was not academic, it was existential,"

Walker said. He listed Thomas Helwys, Roger Williams, Obadiah Holmes, John Leland, and Isaac Backus as among the "pantheon of early Baptist freedom fighters."

But this freedom gifted by God is protected by political and constitutional institutions, he said.

The framers of the U.S. Constitution had a vision for our national government that differed greatly from the example provided by the Puritans, who came to New England in search of religious freedom. "What they gained for themselves, they denied to others," Walker said.

The framers drafted and approved a document that only spoke of religion once—and that was to ban religious tests for public office—and Walker pointed out that it never mentions Christianity. "[W]ith the adoption of the First Amendment's religion clauses in the Bill of Rights ('Congress shall make no law respecting an establishment of religion, or prohibiting the free exercise thereof'), our founders made it clear that one's status in the civil community would not depend on a willingness to sign on the dotted line of any religious confession," Walker said.

Walker stressed that the nation's founders, supported by Baptists and armed with Enlightenment values, fought for robust protection for religious liberty in the U.S. Constitution.

"Some today in the religious community, even the progressive Baptist community, see our current drive to perpetuate religious freedom and church-state separation to be rooted only in the Enlightenment, not theology or biblical principles," Walker said.

But Baptists "got it" long before the Enlightenment thinkers did, he said, and that continues today.

The First Amendment's religion clauses prevent the establishment of religion and forbid interference with the exercise of religion. Both are equally important and must be taken seriously as well as rigorously enforced if we are to adequately protect our religious liberty, Walker said.

In his second lecture, Walker suggested that religious freedom is threatened by a belief that religious disputes should be settled by majority vote.

"Although majoritarian principles are fundamental in a democracy—that's how we settle most political and policy issues—the Bill of Rights generally and the First Amendment's religion clauses in particular are 'counter-majoritarian,'" Walker said. "They ensure the rights of minorities and protect against political majorities."

He said religious liberty is best ensured when government treats religion differently, with special concessions and imposing on religion unique constraints.

Walker explained that religion and religious institutions often are given special accommodations from the government to lift burdens on the free exercise of religion. For example, a Baptist church is allowed to hire a Baptist music director instead of a Buddhist, while for-profit businesses cannot discriminate on the basis of religion in hiring, Walker said. And houses of worship are exempt from having to install ramps and elevators under the Americans with Disabilities Act, while a hotel chain must comply.

On the other hand, sometimes religion must endure unique constraints to prevent the establishment of religion or to ensure compliance with Establishment Clause values, Walker said. Public school teachers can say the Pledge of Allegiance, recite the Gettysburg Address, and express many other things in a classroom, but they may not lead in prayer or religious exercises, Walker said. Also, government may fund many things, including the public schools, but it should not directly fund religion or religious schools. "These limitations on religion operate to ensure government neutrality and promote religious liberty for all, especially religious minorities," he said.

Turning to a controversial issue involving religious exemptions and government accommodations, Walker discussed the Affordable Care Act, the new health care law requiring employers with at least fifty employees to provide insurance coverage, including contraception for female employees.

He said the Baptist Joint Committee initially criticized the presidential administration's failure to offer broader accommodation for religiously affiliated employers with conscience-based objections to contraception, while exempting churches and other houses of worship.

Walker said the administration announced a modified policy in 2012, seeking to balance the conscience rights of religiously affiliated employers who object to forms of contraception and the public interest of ensuring all women have access to preventative health care. And earlier in 2013, the administration announced additional rules to clarify and expand the definition of "religious employer," detailing the process by which self-insured employers would be required to allow a third party administrator to work with health insurers to extend contraception coverage while providing some distance between the objecting employer and the employee desirous of contraception coverage.

Walker concluded his discussion of religious accommodation with a call for a "golden rule" for church-state relations.

"I cannot ask government to promote my religion if I don't want government to promote somebody else's religion; and I cannot permit government to hinder somebody else's religion if I don't want government to hinder my religion," Walker said.

The third lecture concentrated on a common misconception about American public life. That is, the separation of church and state requires a complete separation of religion from politics and a public square stripped of religious discourse.

Not so, Walker said. "The question is not whether religious people will be involved in politics, but how should they do it," he said, and conversations about religion can be a positive force in politics.

"When candidates talk about their faith it can help us know who they are, learn what makes them tick, and examine their moral core," Walker said. "The free and fluid discussion of candidates' faith carries the promise of improving the electorate's ability to make an informed decision in the voting booth."

He then suggested that with those benefits, danger also lurks when we try to combine religion and politics. Walker mentioned several limitations and cautions about the intersection of religion and politics. For example, if a candidate's religion is introduced, the question of how his or her religious views will impact public policy positions and leadership competence is vital.

Other words of caution to the general proposition that religion can be helpful to public discourse included that any foray into politics with focused religious motivation should be tempered with a dose of humility. The second caution dealt with the use or abuse of "civil religion"—or as Walker described it, the "blending of a generic Judeo-Christian piety with American patriotism to the point that one can't tell them apart." The third cautioned churches and other nonprofits from supporting or opposing candidates for public office, which could jeopardize their tax-exempt status.

As for the 2012 elections, Walker was pleased with the way religion and politics mingled.

"With rare exception, we did a commendable job in balancing the pertinence of religion to public life with the prohibition on religious tests," Walker said.

He pointed out that the outcomes in congressional races showcased Americans' growing appreciation for religious diversity. In 2012, the two Muslim members of the U.S. House of Representatives were re-elected, and a Hindu and "religiously unaffiliated" member were also elected to the chamber. The past election also saw the first Buddhist elected to the U.S. Senate. This religious diversity and a society that appears to have come to terms with lawmakers who are neither Christian nor Jewish taking oaths on their own holy books give cause for optimism, Walker concluded.

Churches and Political Campaigns

By K. Hollyn Hollman

(K. Hollyn Hollman is general counsel for the Baptist Joint Committee for Religious Liberty. This information is taken largely from *Tax Guide for Churches and Religious Organizations, Internal Revenue Service publication 1828 (Rev. 9-2003)*. To download the publication as a pdf document, visit www.BJConline.org/electioneering. This general guidance in a complicated area of law does not govern all conceivable issues. For legal advice or specific inquiries, consult with a lawyer directly.)

Each campaign season, we are reminded of the many issues that challenge our nation. As Christians and citizens, we are called to engage the issues, to seek justice, and to elect leaders who we believe best reflect our values and goals. Campaigns also bring questions about the legal boundaries for churches under the tax laws. The following summary reflects available guidance from the Internal Revenue Service. (See *Tax Guide for Churches and Religious Organizations, Internal Revenue Service publication 1828 (Rev. 9-2003)*.)

1. When churches get involved in political issues, don't they necessarily violate the constitutional separation of church and state?

No. The First Amendment's religion clauses do not prohibit political activity by churches. In fact, the First Amendment protects the religious expression of churches in many ways, including their right to speak out on important issues. Churches, however, like other organizations that are exempt from taxes under the Internal Revenue Code Section 501(c)(3) and are eligible to receive tax-deductible contributions, must abide by certain restrictions on lobbying and campaign activity to retain the special treatment they receive under the tax laws.

2. Are the IRS restrictions on participating in campaigns for elected office different from those that limit the amount of lobbying allowed by religious organizations?

Yes. While the Internal Revenue Code limits the amount of activity a tax-exempt organization can devote to attempting to influence legislation (no substantial part of the organization's activity can be devoted to lobbying), it actually bans intervention in political campaigns. As stated in the IRS Tax Guide on this topic: "Under the Internal Revenue Code, all IRC Section 501(c)(3) organizations, including churches and religious organizations, are *absolutely prohibited* from directly or indirectly participating in, or intervening in, any political campaign on behalf of (or in opposition to) any candidate for elective public office. Contributions to political campaign funds or public statements of position (verbal or written) made by or on behalf of the organization in favor of or in opposition to any candidate for public office clearly violate the prohibition against political campaign activity" (p.7., emphasis added).

3. Does the political campaign prohibition mean that church pastors cannot be involved in politics without jeopardizing their church's tax status?

No. The ban on political campaign activity is not intended to restrict the free expression of church leaders speaking for themselves, as individuals. Nor are the rules intended to keep such leaders from speaking about important issues of public policy from the pulpit. "However, for their organizations to remain tax exempt under IRC section 501(c)(3), religious leaders cannot make partisan comments in official organization publications or at official church functions.

To avoid potential attribution of their comments outside of church functions and publications, religious leaders who speak or write in their individual capacity are encouraged to clearly indicate that their comments are personal and not intended to represent the views of the organization" (p. 7). Church leaders should be particularly careful not to endorse candidates in sermons, church bulletins, or other communication channels of the organization.

4. Does the political campaign prohibition mean that churches cannot allow candidates to speak at church events?

No. "Depending on the facts and circumstances, a church or religious organization may invite political candidates to speak at its events without jeopardizing its tax-exempt status. Political candidates may be invited in their capacity as candidates, or individually (not as a candidate)" (p. 8). If a candidate is invited to speak at a church event as a candidate, the church must take steps to ensure that it demonstrates no bias for or against the candidate. For example, the church should provide an equal opportunity for all candidates seeking the same office, avoid indicating support for or opposition to the candidate, and make sure no political fundraising occurs.

Religion in Political Campaigns—
An Interfaith Statement of Principles

(This statement, released February 21, 2012, was drafted by the Baptist Joint Committee for Religious Liberty, the Anti-Defamation League, and the Interfaith Alliance. It calls on all candidates for public office to help ensure decency, honesty, and fair play in elections by conducting campaigns that honor our nation's traditions of religious liberty and avoid sowing religious discord.)

Freedom of religion is one of our nation's most cherished liberties. It is at the very foundation of America. Our nation's Constitution protects religious freedom for all, prohibits religious tests for public office, and mandates separation of church and state. These are essential American ideals and values, which candidates for public office should respect.

Candidates for public office are, of course, free to worship as they choose. And they should feel comfortable explaining their religious convictions to voters, commenting about their own religious beliefs, explaining, if they wish to do so, how those beliefs shape their policy perspectives, and how they would balance the principles of their faith with their obligation to defend the Constitution if the two ever came into conflict.

There is a point, however, where an emphasis on religion in a political campaign becomes inappropriate and even unsettling in a religiously diverse society such as ours. Appealing to voters along religious lines is divisive. It is contrary to the American ideal of including all Americans in the political process, regardless of whether they are members of large and powerful religious groups, religious minorities, or subscribe to no faith tradition.

Voters should be encouraged to make their decisions based upon their assessment of the qualifications, integrity, and political positions of candidates. A candidate's religious beliefs—or lack thereof—should never be used by voters, nor suggested by political candidates, as a test for public office or as a shorthand summary of a candidate's qualifications.

Candidates for office bear the primary responsibility for setting the proper tone for elections. Anyone who legitimately aspires to public office must be prepared to set an example and to be a leader for all Americans, of all faiths or of no faith.

What is ethical is every bit as important as what is legal. Therefore, candidates for public office should:

• Attempt to fulfill the promise of America by seeking to serve and be responsive to the full range of constituents, irrespective of their religion.
• Conduct their campaigns without appeals, overt or implicit, for support based upon religion.
• Reject appeals or messages to voters that reflect religious prejudice, bias, or stereotyping.
• Engage in vigorous debate on important and disputed issues, without deliberately encouraging division in the electorate along religious lines, or between voters who characterize themselves as religious and voters who do not.

Abiding by these principles, candidates for public office help ensure decency, honesty, and fair play in political campaigns, and they honor America's oldest and most fundamental values. Likewise, voters who insist on adherence to these principles contribute to the protection of our religious freedom.

Signed:
American Islamic Congress
American Jewish Committee
Anti-Defamation League
Baptist Joint Committee for Religious Liberty
Interfaith Alliance
Islamic Society of North America (ISNA)
Hindu American Foundation
Muslim Advocates

National Council of Churches USA
Sikh American Legal Defense and Education Fund (SALDEF)
Sikh Coalition
Union for Reform Judaism
The United Methodist Church—General Board of Church and Society
United Church of Christ, Justice and Witness Ministries

www.ingramcontent.com/pod-product-compliance
Lightning Source LLC
LaVergne TN
LVHW021545080426
835509LV00019B/2844